To My Daughter with Love
on the Important Things in Life

Special Updated Edition with New Poems

To Janice

With Much Love,

Mom

Other books by

Susan Polis Schutz

Come Into the Mountains, Dear Friend
Don't Be Afraid to Love
Find Happiness in Everything You Do
Having a Baby Is a Beautiful Miracle of Love and Life
I Love You
I Want to Laugh, I Want to Cry
Love, Live & Share
One World, One Heart
Peace Flows from the Sky
Take Charge of Your Body
by Susan Polis Schutz and Katherine F. Carson, M.D.
To My Son, with Love
Yours If You Ask

To My Daughter with Love

on the Important Things in Life

Special Updated Edition with New Poems

Susan Polis Schutz

Designed and Illustrated by
Stephen Schutz

Blue Mountain Press ™

Boulder, Colorado

ISBN: 0-88396-636-0 (trade paper) — ISBN: 0-88396-452-X (hardcover)

Manufactured in the United States of America.
Sixth Printing trade paperback: 2003

Certain trademarks are used under license.

♲ This book is printed on recycled paper.

This book is printed on fine quality, laid embossed, 80 lb. paper. This paper has been specially produced to be acid free (neutral pH) and contains no groundwood or unbleached pulp. It conforms with all the requirements of the American National Standards Institute, Inc., so as to ensure that this book will last and be enjoyed by future generations.

Library of Congress Cataloging-in-Publication Data

Schutz, Susan Polis.
    To my daughter with love : on the important things in life /
Susan Polis Schutz ; designed and illustrated by Stephen Schutz. —
Special updated ed.
        p.   cm.
    ISBN 0-88396-452-X (hardcover : alk. paper)
    ISBN 0-88396-636-0 (trade paper : alk. paper)
    1. Mothers and daughters—Poetry. 2. Conduct of life—Poetry.
I. Schutz, Stephen. II. Title.
PS3569.C556T6 1997
811'.54—dc21   97-18572
                                                          CIP

Blue Mountain Arts, Inc.
P.O. Box 4549, Boulder, Colorado 80306

CONTENTS

This book is dedicated and written with a lot of
love to my beautiful daughter, Jordanna Polis Schutz,
and to my outstanding mother, June Polis,
on the special occasion of her retirement.

I also want to express my deepest love
to my two wonderful sons, Jared and Jorian,
and of course to my perfect partner
in life and love, Stephen.

INTRODUCTION

When I gave birth to my daughter, Jordanna, I never knew what a special relationship a mother and daughter could have. As my daughter got older and started to understand more about being a female, I felt as if I were once again going through the many stages of growing up. I felt a very strong urge to protect Jordanna from anything that could possibly hurt her, but I knew that if I did this, it would hurt her later on because she would not be prepared to face the real world. So instead, I tried to show her and explain to her what I consider to be the important things in life.

Our mother-daughter relationship is comprised of a very deep understanding of and support for each other, and it is based on an enormous amount of emotion and love. There is no other relationship in the world where two women are so much like one.

Susan Polis Schutz
Introduction to original edition (1985)

When I originally wrote this book, my daughter was just a little girl. Now all of a sudden she has grown into a beautiful young woman who is about to leave home for college.

The emotions surrounding this passage of time with Jordanna have led me to write new poems, which are included in this special updated edition of *To My Daughter with Love*. It chronicles my philosophy, my worries, my love and my deepest feelings towards Jordanna, from when she was an infant through her high-school years.

Next year, when Jordanna is away from home, this book will remind her that it doesn't matter where she is, because home is where love and the heart reside.

Susan Polis Schutz (1997)

To My Daughter

My day becomes wonderful
when I see your
pretty face smiling so sweetly
There is such warmth and intelligence
radiating from you
It seems that every day
you grow smarter and more beautiful
and every day
I am more proud of you
As you go through different stages of life
you should be aware that there will be many times
when you will feel scared and confused
but with your strength and values
you will always end up wiser
and you will have grown from your experiences
understanding more about people and life
I have already gone through
these stages
So if you need advice or someone to talk to
to make sense out of it all
I hope that you will talk to me
as I am continually cheering for your happiness
my sweet daughter
and I love you

To My Daughter, with Love,
on the Important Things in Life

A mother tries to provide her daughter
with insight into the important things in life
in order to make her life
as happy and fulfilling as possible

A mother tries to teach her daughter
to be good, helpful to other people
to be fair, always treating others equally
to have a positive attitude at all times
to make things right when they are wrong
to know herself well
to know what her talents are
to set goals for herself
to not be afraid of working too hard to reach her goals...

(continued)

...A mother tries to teach her daughter
   to have many interests to pursue
   to laugh and have fun every day
   to appreciate the beauty of nature
   to enter into friendships with good people
   to honor their friendships and always be a true friend
   to appreciate the importance of the family
   and to particularly respect and love our elder members
   to use her intelligence at all times
   to listen to her emotions
   to adhere to her values

   A mother tries to teach her daughter
   to not be afraid to stick to her beliefs
   to not follow the majority when the majority is wrong
   to always realize that she is a woman
      equal to all men
   to carefully plan a life for herself
   to vigorously follow her chosen path
   to enter into a relationship with someone worthy of herself
   to love this person unconditionally with her body and mind
   to share all that she has learned in life with this person...

If I have provided you with an insight
into most of these things
then I have succeeded
as a mother
in what I hoped to accomplish in raising you
If some of these things slipped by
while we were all so busy
I have a feeling that you know them anyway
And I certainly hope that you always
   continue to know
how much love and admiration
I have for you
my beautiful daughter

I love you every minute of every day,
my beautiful daughter

*I looked at you today
and saw the same beautiful eyes
that looked at me with love
when you were a baby
I looked at you today
and saw the same beautiful mouth
that made me cry when you first smiled at me
when you were a baby
It was not long ago
that I held you in my arms
long after you fell asleep
and I just kept rocking you
all night long
I looked at you today
and saw my beautiful daughter
no longer a baby
but a beautiful person
with a full range of emotions and feelings
and ideas and goals
Every day is exciting
as I continue to watch you grow
And I want you to always know that
in good and in bad times
I will love you
and that no matter what you do
or how you think
or what you say
you can depend on
my support, guidance
friendship and love
every minute of every day
I love being your mother*

I love you so much, my beautiful daughter
I wish that you could see yourself
as others see you —
a sensitive, pretty, loving, intelligent person
who has all the qualities necessary to
become a very successful and beautiful woman
yet sometimes you seem to
have a low opinion of yourself
You compare yourself unfavorably
to others
I wish that you would only judge yourself
according to your own standards
and not be so hard on yourself
I look forward to the day when
you look in the mirror
and for the first time in your life
you see the extraordinary person
that you really are
and you realize how much
you are loved and appreciated
I love you so much
my beautiful daughter
forever as your mother
and friend

*I hope that you
will have as much
confidence in yourself
as we have in you.*

The True Meaning of Friendship

Some people will be your friend
because of whom you know
Some people will be your friend
because of your position
Some people will be your friend
because of the way you look
Some people will be your friend
because of your possessions
But the only real friends
are the people who will be your friends
because they like you for how you are inside

Try to choose your friends carefully. Make sure that they are worthy of you.

know that lately you
have been having problems
and I just want you to know
that you can rely on me
for anything
you might need
But more important
keep in mind at all times
that you are very capable
of dealing with any complications
that life has to offer
So
do whatever you must
feel whatever you must
and keep in mind
that we all
grow wiser and
become more sensitive and
are able to enjoy life more
after we go through
hard times

*M*y dear daughter
you have come out of a time
mingled with problems
wiser, happier
and much smarter
I am so proud of the way
you handled yourself
the way you thought out the proper solutions
and the strength you used in following through
I no longer have to worry about you
You are very capable of leading your own life
and I know any decisions
that you make for yourself
will be right
You can't imagine how happy this makes me
You are a wonderful person and
a beautiful daughter
I love you dearly

ove is
being happy for the other person
when that person is happy
being sad for the other person
when that person is sad
being together in good times
and being together in bad times
Love is the source of strength

Love is
being honest with yourself at all times
being honest with the other person at all times
telling, listening, respecting the truth
and never pretending
Love is the source of reality

Love is
an understanding so complete that
you feel as if you are a part
of the other person
accepting that person
just the way he or she is
and not trying to change each other
to be something else
Love is the source of unity

Love is
the freedom to pursue your own desires
while sharing your experiences
with the other person
the growth of one individual alongside of
and together with the growth
of another individual
Love is the source of success

Love is
   the excitement of planning things together
   the excitement of doing things together
Love is the source of the future

Love is
   the fury of the storm
   the calm in the rainbow
Love is the source of passion

Love is
   giving and taking in a daily situation
   being patient with each other's
      needs and desires
Love is the source of sharing

Love is
   knowing that the other person
   will always be with you
      regardless of what happens
   missing the other person when he or she is away
   but remaining near in heart at all times
Love is the source of security

Love is
   the
   source
   of
   life

Love is the most important emotion that you will ever have. I hope that you are able to open yourself up to a beautiful love. I have tried to express what love means to me. You will discover your own meaning.

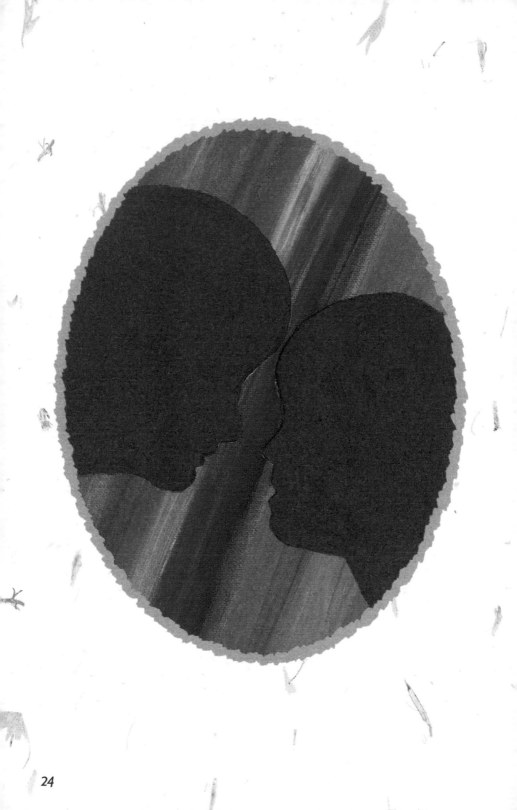

Finding the right person to love
is so important
Love comes naturally
but you must both work
at making it last
and try your hardest
at all times
to be fair and honest with each other

Strive for your own goals
and help your mate achieve his
Always try to understand him
Always let him know what you are thinking
Always try to support him
Try to successfully blend
your lives together
with enough freedom
to grow as individuals
Always consider each day you spend together
as a special day
Regardless of what events
occur in your lives
make sure that your
relationship always flourishes
and that you always
love and respect each other

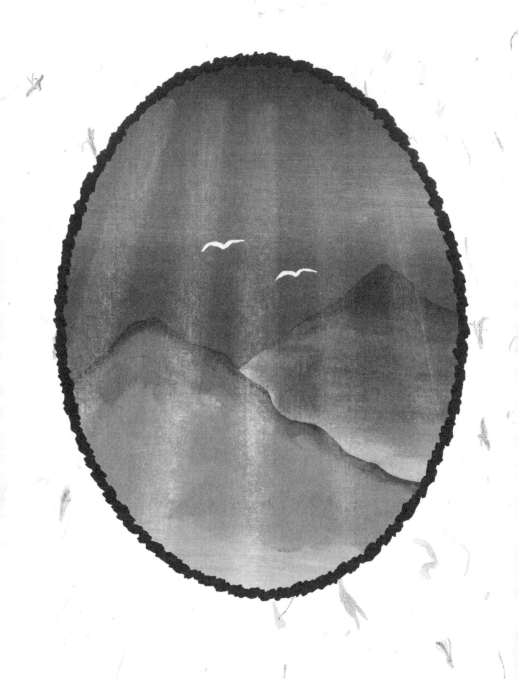

Don't be afraid
to love someone
totally and completely
Love is the most fulfilling
and beautiful feeling in the world
Don't be afraid that you will
get hurt
or that the other person
won't love you
There is a risk in
everything you do
and the rewards
are never so great
as what love can bring
So let yourself get involved
completely and honestly
and enjoy the possibility
that what happens
might be the only real
source of happiness

My darling daughter
I am glad that
you were born in an age
when women are
aware of what is going on
and don't always have
to fight so hard to be heard
The world is wide open
for you to be whatever you want
It will be hard
but at least you
will find other women
striving for the same thing
and you won't be called "crazy"
for wanting to achieve your goals
Though full equality
is not here yet
there certainly have been changes
that will make your life as a woman
not so stereotyped and confined
You are living in an age
where womanhood is
finally growing
to be everything
that it can be
My darling daughter
I have watched you play with
dolls and trucks
footballs and toads
and I picture you
my beautiful child
as a beautiful woman
in full control of her life

It is very difficult
for a woman
to have a
successful career and
happy children and an
exciting personal life

When attending to work
most women feel guilty
because they are not with their children
When attending to their children
most women feel guilty
because they have work to do
And if there is time
for personal things
most women feel guilty
because they are neither
attending to the needs of their children
nor their work

In order for a woman
to successfully do
all the things she wants to
she must delegate the things
she does not want to do —
and her husband must equally
share family responsibilities
Otherwise
all the demands on the woman
leave her too tired and frustrated
to enjoy life
And that just isn't fair

Many women
I have talked to lately
tell me that they are
extremely unfulfilled
being housewives
that their work all day
is so unimportant
that they are not using
their minds —
These women must
do something that
interests them
but they must also
be reassured that
being a good mother is an
extremely important job
and that just because society
seems to say that raising children
is a menial task
there is no reason to believe this
In fact many beliefs that society
imposes on the individual
are wrong
Women must realize
that whatever they do
is important
as long as they do it well

A woman will get only what she seeks
Choose your goals carefully
Know what you like
and what you do not like
Be critical about what you can do well
and what you cannot do well
Choose a career or lifestyle that interests you
and work hard to make it a success
but also have fun in what you do
Be honest with people
   and help them if you can
but don't depend on anyone
   to make life easy or happy for you
(only you can do that for yourself)
Be strong and decisive
but remain sensitive
Regard your family, and the idea of family
as the basis for security, support and love
Understand who you are
and what you want in life
before sharing your life with someone
When you are ready to enter a relationship
make sure that the person is worthy of
everything you are physically and mentally
Strive to achieve all that you want
Find happiness in everything you do
Love with your entire being
Love with an uninhibited soul
Make a triumph
of every aspect
of your life

Find happiness in everything you do.

We cannot
listen to what
others want us
to do
We must listen
to ourselves
We don't need to
copy other people's ways
and we don't need to
act out certain lifestyles
to impress other people
Only we know
and only we can do what
is right for us
So start right now
You will need to
work very hard
You will need to
overcome many obstacles
You will need to go
against the better
judgment of many people
and you will need to
bypass their prejudices
But you can have
whatever you want
if you try hard enough
Start right now so that
you can live a life
designed by you and
for you —
a life you deserve

Only you
can choose the
lifestyle you
want to
follow.

Live Your World of Dreams

ean against a tree
and dream your world of dreams
Work hard at what you like to do
and try to overcome all obstacles
Laugh at your mistakes
and praise yourself for learning from them
Pick some flowers
and appreciate the beauty of nature
Be honest with people
and enjoy the good in them
Don't be afraid to show your emotions
Laughing and crying make you feel better
Love your friends and family with your entire being
They are the most important part of your life
Feel the calmness on a quiet sunny day
and plan what you want to accomplish in life
Find a rainbow
and live your
world of dreams
I love you

Always have dreams.
Always try to make
them a reality.

You Are One of Those Rare People
Whose Dreams Will Become a Reality

What makes people succeed
is the fact that they have confidence in themselves
and a very strong sense of purpose
They never have excuses for not doing something
and always try their hardest for perfection
They never consider the idea of failing
and they work extremely hard towards their goals
They know who they are
and they understand their weaknesses
as well as their strong points
They can accept and benefit from criticism
and they know when to defend what they are doing
They are creative people
who are not afraid to be a little different
You are one of these rare people
and it is so exciting to watch you
on your path to success
as you follow your dreams
and make them a reality

I Am Always Here for You

I suspect that
you are thinking about something
that is bothering you
Please share any problems
that you might be having
with someone (it doesn't matter with whom)
because if you just keep these problems in your mind
you will not be able to pursue
your thoughts and activities
to your fullest potential
nor will you be able to enjoy
all the great things in life
because problems, whether they are large or small
often dominate one's thoughts
You are such a wonderful person
and you should always be happy
and free from nagging worries

I want to remind you that
I am always ready to
listen to you in an understanding way
so if you ever need me
I am always here for you

Sometimes I talk to you
and I am not really sure
what you are thinking
It is so important
to let your feelings
be known
Talk to someone
Write your feelings down
Create something based on your feelings
but do not keep them inside
Never be afraid to
be honest with people
and certainly never be afraid to
be honest with yourself
You are such an
interesting, sensitive, intelligent person
who has so much to share
I want you to know
that wherever you go
or whatever you do
or whatever you think
you can always depend
on me, your mother
for complete and absolute
understanding
support
and love
forever

lder people
could teach us
so much
if we would
only listen
Their wisdom
their simplicity
their experiences
their many years of living
We need them to
live with us
with our families
to teach us
and our children
all they know
to love us
and to let us
love them
and to let us
help them
when they
need it
A family
is not complete
without its
eldest
members

*The love
of a family
is so
uplifting*

*The warmth
of a family
is so
comforting*

*The support
of a family
is so reassuring*

*The attitude
of a family
towards
each other
molds one's
attitude forever
towards the
world*

I Want You to Live a Life of Love, My Daughter

We brought you into this world
a beautiful little girl
born of love
who would one day
grow up to be
a beautiful woman full of love

I tried to teach you
important values and morals
I tried to show you
how to be strong and honest, gentle and sensitive
I tried to explain to you
the importance of achieving your own goals
I tried to express
the need to reach out to people
I tried to emphasize
the beauty of nature
I tried to demonstrate
the extreme importance of family
And I tried, every day, to set an example
that you could look up to

When we brought you into the world
I did not think about how everything
could be destroyed in a few minutes
in a world not at peace
in a world with nuclear weapons

I taught you love
in a sometimes hateful world
because it is love that can abolish hate
before hate abolishes us

I am very sorry, my beautiful daughter
that these destructive forces
have been handed down to you
All of the mothers
and all of the fathers
in the entire world
must unite together and
dedicate ourselves to
ending violence as a way
of solving problems
We must do this so that we can assure you
my daughter, and all children
that you will grow up
to hike in the mountains
and run in the fields of flowers
so that we can assure you
that you will have a chance to grow up
to live a life
of peace and
love

You are a shining
example of what a
daughter can be —
loving and compassionate
beautiful and good
honest and principled
determined and independent
sensitive and intelligent
You are a shining
example of what every
mother wishes her
daughter were
and I
am so very
proud of
you

If you know yourself well
and have developed a sense
of confidence in yourself
If you are honest with yourself
and honest with others
If you follow your heart
and adhere to your own truths
you are ready to share yourself
you are ready to set goals
you are ready to find happiness
And the more you love
and the more you give
and the more you feel
the more you will receive
from love
and the more you will receive
from life

The freer you are
with your emotions
and feelings, the more you
will be able to give and
receive love.

Sometimes you
think that you
need to be perfect
that you cannot
make mistakes
At these times
you put so much
pressure on yourself
I wish that you
would realize
that you are
like everyone else —
capable of
reaching great potential
but not capable of
being perfect
So please
just do your best
and realize that
this is enough
Don't compare yourself
to anyone
Be happy to be
the wonderful
unique, very special
person that you are

A friend is
someone who is concerned
with everything you do

A friend is
someone who is concerned
with everything you think

A friend is
someone to call upon
during good times

A friend is
someone to call upon
during bad times

A friend is
someone who understands
whatever you do

A friend is
someone who tells you the truth
about yourself

A friend is
someone who knows
what you are going through at all times

A friend is
someone who refuses to listen
to gossip about you

A friend is
someone who supports you
at all times

A friend is
someone who does not
compete with you

A friend is
someone who is genuinely happy for you
when things go well

A friend is
someone who tries to cheer you up
when things don't go well

A friend is
an extension of yourself
without which
you are not complete

Everyone needs people to
understand them throughout
life. I hope that you have at least
one good friend for life. I
have tried to define what a
friend is to me...

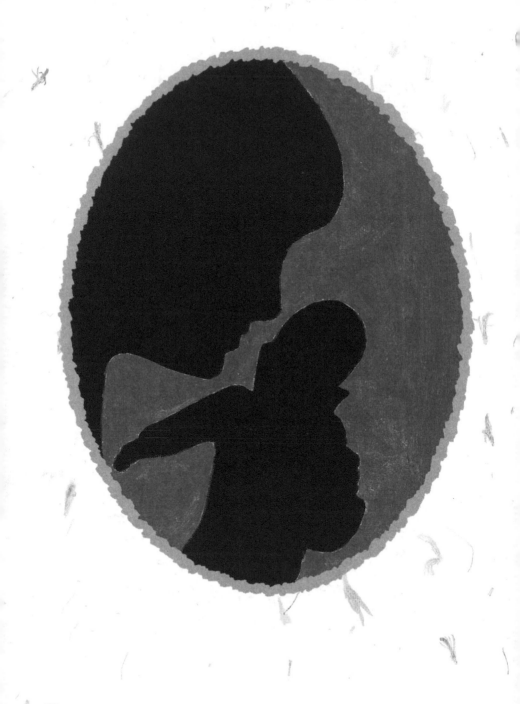

My Daughter

Since you were born
you have been
such a beautiful
addition to our family
Now that you are growing up
I can see that
you are a beautiful
addition to the world
and I am so
proud of you
As I watch you
doing things on your own
I know you will find
happiness and success
because I am confident in
your ability
your self-knowledge
your values
But if you ever need a boost
or just someone to talk to
I am always here
to help you
to understand you
to support you
and to love
you

I Love Your Beautiful Smile,
My Daughter

Sometimes I see you
confused
Sometimes I see you
troubled
Sometimes I see you
hurt
and I feel so sad and
helpless
I wish that I could absorb
these feelings from you
and make everything better
but I know that these feelings
will only help you to grow
and understand more about life
These feelings will help you
to become a more sensitive person
So as I watch your eyes
which tell me everything
I will offer you my
understanding and support
I will offer you my
tears and love
I will offer you the
promise that your beautiful
smile will soon return

My daughter
when you were born
I held you in my arms
and just kept smiling at you
You always smiled back
your big eyes wide open
full of love
Now
as I watch you grow up
and become your own person
I look at you
your laughter
your happiness
your simplicity
your beauty
and I wonder where you will be
in fifteen years
and I wonder
where the world will be
in fifteen years
I just hope that you will
be able to enjoy a life
of sensitivity
goodness
accomplishment
and love
in a world that is at peace
But most of all
I want you to know that
I am very proud of you
and that I love you dearly

What Is a Daughter?

daughter is
a rainbow bubble
a star glimmering in the sky
a rosebud after a storm
a caterpillar turning into a butterfly

A daughter is
hair flying in the wind
red cheeks that glisten in the sunshine
big daydream eyes

A daughter is
a wonder
a sweetness, a secret, an artist
a perception, a delight

You are all these things
and so much more
You are everything that is beautiful
I love you

To My Daughter, I Love You

So many times
   you ask me questions
     and your big beautiful eyes
       look at me
        with trust, confusion and
      innocence
I always hope that my
answers to you
will help guide you
Even though I always want to protect you
and step in for you when you have a
   difficult decision to make
it is very important that I do not interfere
so that you will learn from your own experiences
and develop confidence in your own judgment
There is a fine line between
a mother telling her daughter
too much
or too little
I hope I have struck a proper balance
I have always wanted to tell you
how honored I am that you
seek out my opinions
I appreciate the trust you have in me and
I want you to know that
I have an immense trust in you
I am very proud of you
as I watch you growing up to be an
intelligent, independent, sensitive young woman
I love you

Ever since you were born
you have been a bundle of
perpetual motion
Your energy is endless
Your mind is unbounded
You want to touch, smell, feel and do everything
You want to live life to the fullest
But don't forget
you are extraordinarily creative
and it is hard for creativity to flourish
unless there is a certain amount
of quietness and peace
So you will, at times, need to quell
your vigor
stop your movements
and let the perpetual motion of your mind
leap to new bounds
as you bask in the stillness of your
spirit and soul

ou have continually
demonstrated your
incredible intelligence, creativity
and ability to work very hard
Your accomplishments
have soared
You have risen
to heights
way beyond your years
I am so proud of you
Your noble morals —
despite the way of the world
Your strength —
while many people are weak
And your sensitivity —
when many people are uncaring
You are a very special individual
because you are able to
stick so firmly to your principles
I think you have discovered
who you are, however —
I want to be sure that
you are in touch
with your heart and emotions
as well as your intellect
so that you will be
able to develop the kinds
of close relationships that
together with your accomplishments
will make you truly happy

Your soft sensitive side
will need to blend with your
worldly side
And you will need to learn to
ignore the mean words of others
as well as their excessive praises
You, not other people
must be the judge of your life
And in the future
I hope you can spend
more time being free
to do what you want
You are a very creative spirit
who needs to fly more
I love the
respect and friendship that
we have discovered
with each other
It is so much fun
talking and going places
with you
We have a lot in common —
often seeing things
no one else notices
smelling things
no one else smells
observing and understanding people's obscure
peculiarities and characteristics
I enjoy being with you, Princess
and I love you

I remember so well
when you were eleven months old and
you jumped over your high crib wall
and happily ran to my room
delighted in your new-found freedom
I remember so well
your soft bouncy hair
falling over your huge inquisitive eyes
your little rosebud lips quietly
chuckling at things you found funny
and your sunny red cheeks
against your porcelain baby face...
That was sixteen years ago
and though it seems so long ago
you are the same now
only taller and older
Your hair still
falls over your enormous eyes —
eyes that twinkle with
intelligence and innocence
Your little rosebud lips speak
with big sophisticated words and ideas
and often chuckle in a cynical way
at things you find funny
Your cheeks are red from
outdoor sports
and your skin is still
so soft and delicate

And now
your quest for freedom and happiness
has led you far from your crib
of sixteen years ago
and every day it is taking on new dimensions
as you experiment to find your way
You always work so hard
to do your best
while giving your entire mind and heart
to the new avenues you try
I proudly observe your journey
and I know that wherever it leads you
you will have outstanding successes
and you will have fun, happiness and challenges
because in your intelligent search
for freedom
you will discover
your own
reason for work
significance for your heart
and meaning for your life

My Daughter,
I Am So Proud of You

Every day
I am astounded
to hear you talk
   so intelligently
Your wisdom grows
   and grows
as you do
You are such a delight
such a joy
such a beautiful person
The love I see
   in your eyes for me
is so moving and rewarding
And I hope you
   see and feel
the infinite love I have for you
Whatever you do
wherever you go
always know that
I am here
in every way
for you

I am so glad
that you are able
to be truthful
even when it is very difficult
No matter what you do in life
as long as you are honest
with yourself and others
things will tend to straighten out
You will always be able
to walk with pride
and as a result
your life should be
filled with inner peace and happiness
As your mother
that is what I wish for you
If you ever need someone
to talk to
remember that a
very proud mother
is always ready to listen
without passing judgment
I love you

ou are such an outstanding person
and I hope nothing ever changes
your inner beauty
As you keep growing
remember always
to look at things the way you do now —
with sensitivity
honesty
compassion
and a touch of innocence
Remember that people and situations
may not always be
as they appear
but if you remain true to yourself
things will be all right
With your outlook, you will see
the good in everything
and this will reflect back to you
When I look ahead
I see happiness for you on every level
and I am so glad
because that is what every mother
wishes for her daughter
I love you

I often marvel at your strength
to not give in to current misguided
morals and trends
I look at others your age —
some going through life aimlessly
and I know your journey
must be tough and lonely
because it is hard to be an individual
in a world of followers
where it is easy to go along with the crowd
It is so important for people
to actually choose the way to conduct their lives
And because you have done this
your relationships and accomplishments
will be genuinely deserved
and though there may not be a lot of people
with whom you will feel a kindred spirit
the people you find who are similar to yourself
will be the ones
who stand apart from the crowd
They, like you, are the people
who will make a difference
in the world
with their dreams and actions

You are so modest
that you really don't know or believe
how you are viewed by others
and in a way, that is nice
People respect and admire you
They see you as being extremely
intelligent and knowledgeable
strong and tenacious
creative and innovative
sensitive and kind
moral and honorable
fair and pretty
fun-loving and witty
athletic and vigorous
They see you as
a leader
a thinker
a doer
I think you possess all of
these attributes and more
and you don't even know it
which keeps you unassuming
and in a way, that is nice
Words cannot express
how proud I am of you
Only my heart can show you
how much I love you

To My Wonderful Daughter

To see you happy —
laughing and dancing
smiling and content
striving towards goals of your own
accomplishing what you set out to do
having fun by yourself and with your friends
capable of loving and being loved
is what I always wished for you

Today I thought about your beautiful face
and felt your excitement for life
and your genuine happiness
and I am so proud of you
My dreams for you have come true
What an extraordinary person you are
and as you continue to grow
please remember always
how very much
I love you

Daughter...

*When you need someone
to talk to
I hope you will
talk to me*

*When you need someone
to laugh with
I hope you will
laugh with me*

*When you need someone
to advise you
I hope you will
turn to me*

*When you need someone
to help you
I hope you will
let me help you*

*I cherish and love
everything about you —
my beautiful daughter
And I will always support you
as a mother, as a person
and as a friend*

We Will Be with You Always

This is your last year at home
then to college
new people
new environment
new learning
I know you are
more than ready
to absorb the dazzling knowledge
from the ivory towers
of lofty minds
but are you ready
to leave the familiar
surroundings of your
loving home and
small-town environment?
Don't be afraid
You are so strong
in your beliefs and values that
you will be comfortable
in any situation in which
you find yourself
because you will be in charge —
choosing the best aspects
and avoiding the worst
You are ready, Honey —
Your mind needs new challenges
Your soul needs new like souls
And always remember that
though we will say good-bye for now
your family deeply loves you
Wherever you are
we will be right there with you —
in your dorm, in the library, everywhere you are —
in our minds and in our hearts
I love you

ABOUT THE AUTHORS

Susan began her writing career at the age of seven, producing a neighborhood newspaper for her friends in the small country town of Peekskill, New York, where she was raised. Upon entering her teen years, she began writing poetry as a means of understanding her feelings. For Susan, writing down what she was thinking and feeling brought clarity and understanding to her life, and today she heartily recommends this to everyone. She continued her writing as she attended and graduated from Rider University, where she majored in English and biology. She then entered a graduate program in physiology, while at the same time teaching elementary school in Harlem and contributing freelance articles to newspapers and magazines. Recently, Susan was the recipient of an Honorary Doctor of Laws Degree from Rider University.

Stephen Schutz, a native New Yorker, spent his early years studying drawing and lettering as a student at the High School of Music and Art in New York City. He went on to attend M.I.T., where he received his undergraduate degree in physics. During this time, he continued to pursue his great interest in art by taking classes at the Boston Museum of Fine Art. He later entered Princeton University, where he earned his doctoral degree in theoretical physics.

It was in 1965, at a social event at Princeton, that Susan and Stephen met, and their love affair began. Together, they participated in peace movements and anti-war demonstrations to voice their strong feelings against war and destruction of any kind. They motorcycled around the farmlands of New Jersey and spent many hours outdoors with each other, enjoying their deep love and appreciation of nature. They daydreamed of how life should be.

Susan and Stephen were married in 1969 and moved to Colorado to begin life together in the mountains, where Susan did freelance writing at home and Stephen researched solar energy in a laboratory. On the weekends, they began experimenting with printing Susan's poems, surrounded by Stephen's art, on posters that they silk-screened in their basement. They loved being together so much that it did not take long for them to begin disliking the 9-to-5 weekday separation that had resulted from their pursuing different careers. They soon decided that their being together, not just on weekends but all of the time, was more important than anything else, so Stephen left his research position in the laboratory. They packed their pickup-truck camper with the silk-screened posters they had made, and they began a year of traveling together in the camper and selling their posters in towns and cities across the country. Their love of life and for one another, which so warmly communicate, touched the public. People wanted more of Susan's deep, rich thoughts on life, love, family, friendship, and nature presented in the emotion-stirring colors and rhythmic drawings of Stephen's highly sensitive art. And so, in 1972, in response to incredible public demand, their first book, COME INTO THE MOUNTAINS, DEAR FRIEND, was published, and history was made in the process. Today, after 33 years of marriage and spending all of their time together, Susan and Stephen continue to share their love with all of us.

Besides this book, Susan has authored 10 other bestselling books of poetry. Her poems have been published on over 350 million greeting cards and have appeared in numerous national and international magazines and high-school and college textbooks. She has edited books by other well-known authors and coauthored a woman's health book. Susan writes music and has recorded her poems to the accompaniment of contemplative background music. She is also currently working on her autobiography.

It was the tragic events of September 11, 2001 that led Susan and Stephen to create their newest volume of Susan's poetry and Stephen's artwork, ONE WORLD, ONE HEART. This book is being distributed free to thousands of people throughout the world, with the hope that Susan's words will encourage people everywhere to put aside their differences and come together in peace, understanding, and love.

In addition to designing and illustrating all of Susan's books, Stephen's art complements the words of many other well-known authors. He creates beautiful greeting cards and calendars, which feature his special airbrush and watercolor blends, his beautiful oil paintings, and his unique calligraphy. Stephen is an accomplished photographer and continues to study physics as a hobby. It was his proficiency in the principles of physics that led him in 1993 to create 5-D™ Stereograms, innovative, computer-generated artwork containing hidden, multidimensional images that seem to "come alive." Stephen was recently awarded a patent in this field. He founded and developed the popular World Wide Web site, bluemountainarts.com, where Internet users can personalize and electronically send interactive, animated greeting cards to other users all over the world.

Susan and Stephen have three children. They spend all of their time with their family, including their children in everything that they do. Together, they participate in many outdoor sports, such as hiking in the mountains, swimming in the ocean, and cross-country skiing along the Continental Divide. Half of their time is spent traveling, and the other half is spent working together in their studio in Colorado. Theirs is an atmosphere of joy, love, and spontaneous creativity as they continue to produce the words, the poems, the rhythm, and the art that have reached around the world, opening the hearts and enriching the lives of more than 500 million people in every country, in every language, in every culture. Truly, our world is a happier place because of this perfectly matched and beautifully blended couple, Susan Polis Schutz and Stephen Schutz.

Susan Polis Schutz and Stephen Schutz

Photo by Rocky Thies